Blacks In Mathematics & Science

Workbook 1

Michael Williams

BIS Publications

First Printing: 2016

ISBN **9781903289952**

www.bispublications.com
www.blackscientistsandinventors.com

BIS Publications
PO BOX 14918
London N17 8WJ

Tel:+44(0)7903791469

Ordering Information:

Trade bookstores and wholesalers:
Please contact BIS Publications Tel: +44(0)7903791469; or email info@bispublications.com

Text Copyright © 2016 by Michael Williams
Book cover Copyright © 2016 Cindy Soso

All rights reserved. This book or any portion thereof may not be reproduced or used in any manner whatsoever without the express written permission of the publisher except for the use of brief quotations in a book review or scholarly journal.

How To Use This Book

A note to parents and teachers

Dear parent/educator, this workbook is designed to be used by children between the ages of 5 – 16 years old. It is based on the Black Scientists and Inventors series of books. It is designed to encourage children to practice their investigative, experimental and problem solving skills.

The book is split up into three sections, they are:

1. Science
2. Mathematics
3. Financial Literacy.

In this first title of the '*Blacks In Mathematics and Science: Workbook*' series, we are giving the child a sample of what they'll find in the workbooks series which range from keystage 1 to keystage 4.

It is best for the child to first attempt the questions which are suitable either for the child's keystage or ability, They can then move onto harder questions if they wish.

This workbook will help pupils develop their science, maths, financial and history problem solving skills. It is the author's hope that parents and teachers will also assists the child with this book if needed and help the children on this journey of knowledge and discovery.

Special note to students.

Answers to the questions can be found at the end of this book. However, they are there as a guide, use them only after you have first attempted the questions and used the Black Scientists and Inventors series of books as a guide.

Do not be disappointed if you get some of the answers wrong, remember this is a learning exercise. It is more important that you learn the skills of problem solving and learning from mistakes, so that you can be inspired to do great things in your life. Remember if you cheat, you will only be cheating yourself.

Good Luck and have fun while learning!

Do have fun!

Michael Williams.

Science

Habitats

Key Stages 1 to 3

Experiment No: 1

A woodlouse.

To investigate worms, squirrels and woodlice and find out the following:

Q 1: What is their habitat (where do they live)?, how do they feed?, why do they look and act they way they do?. Have they got feet, claws or neither?, how do they move? and how do they sleep?

What you will need:
A friend or an older brother or sister or a parent to accompany you with a pen and paper.

Method:
Copy the questions above. Visit your school library or search the internet to find the answers to the questions above or when you are in the park, find a Park Ranger and ask him/her the questions.

Results:
Draw a table of your results like the one across the page and fill it in with your findings.

A squirrel.

A worm.

Habitats

Subject	Habitat	Feed by	Reason for looks & actions	Feet / Claws	How do they Move?	How do they Sleep?
Worms						
Squirrels						
Woodlice						

Making Music With Bottles

Key Stages 1 to 2

Experiment No: 2

To investigate sound through musical bottles. You may need an adult assisting you.

What you will need:
Eight empty glass bottles, water, a ruler, 8 labels, pen and paper.

Method:
Use a ruler to measure one side of the bottle and with the marker pen, mark a horizontal line around the first bottle 1cm, repeat this on the remaining bottles at the following heights: 3cm, 6cm, 9cm, 12cm, 15cm, 18cm and 21cm. In each bottle fill up with water to that bottles marker. Bring each bottle to your mouth and blow across the top.

Repeat this experiment, not blowing across the bottle, but firmly taping each bottle with the ruler.

Results:

(a) Record your results in the table on the next page.

(b) Describe the sound you hear?

(c) Does the sound change for the different amounts of water?

(d) If yes, why do you think this is?

Results Continue:

Amount of water in bottle	Description of sound when blowing across bottle top	Description of sound when tapping bottle with a ruler
1cm		
3cm		
6cm		
9cm		
12cm		
15cm		
18cm		
21cm		

Opposites Attract

Key Stages 1 to 2

Experiment No: 3

To investigate the properties of a magnet.

What you will need:
Two rectangular (bar) shaped magnets, a clear flat surface such as a table top, A4 white paper and a ruler.

Method:
Place the A4 paper on the table, then place one magnet on top of it in the middle. Using the ruler measure 10cm from the magnet and then place the second magnet, with the two long ends opposite each other. Slowly move the magnets closer to one another until they meet. Now move the magnets to their original positions and turn one of them clockwise 180 degrees. Once again move the magnets slowly together until they meet.

Results:

Q1: What happened as they moved closer?

Q2: What happened when one of the magnets was turned 180 degrees?

Q3: A magnet has two poles, what are the names of the poles, circle the correct two below.

[North], [East], [South], [West]

Q4: Which of the following cannot be attracted by a magnet?

[Iron], [plastic ruler], [water], [copper coins], [steel fork]

Melting and Boiling Points

Key Stages 1 to 3

Experiment No: 4

To investigate heat transfer and the three states-of-matter.
You must have an adult assist you with this experiment.

What you will need:
A metal pot half full with ice cubes, a thermometer and an electric or gas stove.

Method and results:

Q1: As soon as the ice turns to water, place the thermometer into the water and measure the temperature of the water, what is it?

Q2: Place the pot of water on the stove and turn on the heat. When the water bubbles and there is steam rising from it, turn off the stove. Place the thermometer into the water and measure the temperature, what is it?

Q3: What temperature does the LIQUID water need to be in order to turn to a SOLID such as ice?

Q4: What temperature does the LIQUID water need to be in order to turn to a GAS such as steam?

Did You Know?

Solids, liquids and gases have different properties.

Liquids and gases can flow.
Solids keep their shape.
Gases can be squashed.

Sundial

Key Stages 1 to 3

Experiment No: 5

To investigate **TIME** produced by sunlight.

What you will need:
A safe open space outside, stick or ruler, rocks or stone, a working watch or clock.

Method:
Find a sunny spot outside in the safe open space. Put the stick in the ground, notice that it creates a shadow of the stick. Throughout the day, place a rock, or mark with chalk for each hour indicating where the shadow falls at that time.

Depending on your time, you may have to place rocks over a couple of days before your sundial is complete.

Now your sundial is ready to use. When you want to tell the time, just look for the shadow. You can check your sundial time against your watch / clock.

Results:

Q1: What can you see?

Q2: Find out what is meant by 'Climate Change'?

Q3: Find out what things help to cause Climate Change?

A Sundial using stick and stones.

Heart Beat

Key Stages 1 to 2

Experiment No: 6

To investigate the heart.

What you will need:
You can use either of the following: stopwatch, watch, clock or clock on a mobile/cellular phone.

Method:
You will be testing your heart beat at 3 different conditions.

Q1: Test at rest, that is testing whilst sitting down in a quite room listening to calm music quietly.
Q2: Test whilst walking for 30 minutes.
Q1: Test after you have run 30 meters at your very fastest.

Did You Know?

The first successful open-heart surgery was performed by African American Daniel Hale Williams in 1893.

Results:

Put your results in table below:

Tests	How many times your heart beats in 1 minute.
Whilst at rest (sitting on a chair)	
Immediately after walking for 30 minutes.	
Immediately after running at top speed for 30 metres.	

Conclusion:

All About Our Blood

Key Stages 2 to 4

Investigation No: 1

To investigate what makes up our blood.

To answer the questions below, you may need help from the **'Black Scientists and Inventors Book 6'**

Q1: What is the colour of human blood?

Q2: What is the difference between blood and blood plasma?

Q3: What are the names of the two blood cells found in our blood?

Q4: What is the name of the famous doctor who discovered a method for storing blood safely in a blood bank?

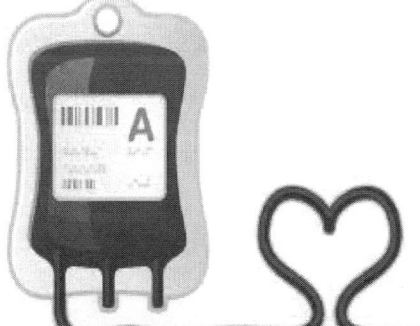

Did You Know?
An adult who weighs between 150 to 180 pounds, body will contain approximately 4.7 to 5.5 litres (1.2 to 1.5 gallons) of blood. Scientist say that the volume of blood in our body is approximately 7 percent of our body weight.

Healthy Eating -
(Food Groups)

Key Stages 2 to 4

Investigation No: 2

To investigate:

Q1: Name the Ugandan doctor and inventor, who invented the food supplement treatment named **Mariandina**?

Q2: When was Mariandina invented?

Q3: What illnesses can it be used to treat?
(**Clue:** For questions 1 to 3, *Look in the Black Scientists & Inventors Books 3 and Book 5*)

Did You Know?

We need a balanced diet in order to have a healthy body. We must drink enough water and eat the right amount of items from the four main food groups.

They are: *carbohydrates, proteins, fats, vitamins and minerals.*

Healthy Eating - (Food Groups)

You will need to get information on the following:
Carbohydrates, Fats & Oils, Proteins and Vitamins & Minerals.

Method:
Either go to your local library or bookshop and ask for books that contain information on food groups. If you can't get hold of a good book on the subject try searching for the information on the internet from sites such as BBC Bite Size.

Results:

	Why we need them	Meats which contain them	Fruits & vegetables which contain them
Carbohydrates			
Fats and Oils			
Proteins			
Vitamins & Minerals			

Inventions and Discoveries

Key Stages 2 to 4

Investigation No: 3

To investigate how much you can remember and understand from reading the Black Scientists & Inventors series of books.

Q1: Who invented the carbon filament light bulb in 1881?

Q2: Who invented a traffic light signalling system in 1923?

Q3: Who is the the real father of medicine?

Q4: In which continent can the country Egypt be found?

Africa [ ], Asia[ ], Europe[ ], America[ ].

Q5: Who built the ancient city Great Zimbabwe?

Greek sailors [ ], African builders [ ], Chinese builders [ ], Aliens [ ].

Q6: Which African American inventor was invited to London in the 1870s to help set up the early electrical light industry?

Q7: In which continent was paper made from papyrus invented and how long ago was this?

Who Am I...?

Key Stages 2 to 3

Investigation No: 4

To investigate how much you can remember and understand from reading the Black Scientists & Inventors series of books.

Q1: I helped Alexander Graham Bell acquire a **patent** for his telephone. This enabled him to become known as the inventor of the telephone. Who am I, and how did I help make the telephone invention possible? [**Clue:** Black Scientists & Inventors Book 1]

Q2: In the 1980s, my company 'Basis Volume', had a 10 year lead in **High Temperature Super Conductor** technology, my inventions were on displayed in the London Science Museum, during that period. Who am I, where was I born and where was my company based? [**Clue:** Black Scientists & Inventors Book 5]

Q3: In 1988 I became the first woman to receive a medical patent for my invention the **Laserphaco Probe ™**. Who am I? [**Clue:** Black Scientists & Inventors Book 4 and 6]

Q4: I am a mix deejay, an inventor and also a professor at Imperial College, London. What do I teach at Imperial college and what is my name? [**Clue:** Black Scientists & Inventors in the UK: Book 5]

Q5: In 1893 a Mr James Cornish entered my hospital with a stab wound to his heart. At the time everyone in the medical industry thought it impossible to operate on a heart without the patient dying. I operated and saved Mr Cornish's life. I became the first person to perform a successful open-heart surgery. What is my name, where and when was I born? [**Clue:** Black Scientists & Inventors Book 6]

Q6: I taught Charles Darwin Taxidermy, who am I and what is Taxidermy? [**Clue:** Black Scientists & Inventors in the UK: Book 5]

Plants

Key Stages 2 to 3

Investigation No: 5

To investigate how plants grow.

Q1: What are the three main things which plants need in order to grow?

Q2: Circle below the counties where bananas grow best?

[England], [Ghana], [Denmark], [France], [Jamaica], [Iceland], [Tanzania]

Q3: What plant does cane sugar come from?

Q4: Circle the countries where sugar cane grows best?

[Mauritius], [Scotland], [Barbados], [Germany], [St Vincent], [Greenland].

Q5: During the trans-atlantic enslavement trade, enslaved Africans made western European countries very wealthy by growing and producing sugar.

a) Can you name 5 Caribbean countries where sugar was grown during the trans-atlantic enslavement trade?

b) What is the process for turning sugar cane into sugar, describe the steps and the instruments used to do so?

Sugar Cane

Animals & Humans

Key Stages 1 to 3

Investigation No: 6

To investigate the differences and similarities between humans and animals.

Q1: What is a clinic or hospital for animals called?

Q2: What are doctors who heal sick animals called?

Q3: Name 5 things which make animals different from human beings?

Q4: On a separate blank paper draw an animal with fur from an African country, name the animal and name the country?

Q5: On a separate paper draw an animal with feathers from a Caribbean country, name the animal and name the country?

Q6: What is animal husbandry?

Q7: What is the difference between a horse and a zebra?

Q8: Which continent are zebras from?

Humans

Q1: Homo sapien (sapien) are modern human beings, they originated in Africa many years ago. Years later some left Africa and travelled and populated the rest of the world. Circle below the correct time period when Homo sapiens first appeared on the earth.

[1 to 2 million years ago], [100,000 – 250,000], [4000 - 6000 years ago],

Q2: Circle below all those which belong to the human family?

[Man], [Dog], [Cub], [Parrot], [Baby], [Kid], [Woman], [Tiger].

Q3: Find out what the words **"Homo erectus and Homo sapien"** mean?

Listening to Light Waves

Key Stages 1 to 2

Investigation No: 7

To investigate **Electricity, Light and Sound.**

Q1: Which of the below uses electricity:

[Radio], [Mobile Phone], [Kettle], [Candle], [Wind Mill], [Light Bulb]

Q2: Which of the below does not produce light?

[The sun], [Clouds], [Candle], [Electric torch], [Fire],

Circle the correct one:

Q1: Sound waves can be seen in the air. [YES] or [NO]

Q2: Our eyes allow us to hear sound. [YES] or [NO]

Q3: Our ears allow us to hear sound. [YES] or [NO]

Q4: Humans can hear higher pitched sounds better than dogs. [YES] or [NO]

Q5: Speech can create sound waves. [YES] or [NO]

Q6: Musical instruments such as drums create sound waves. [YES] or [NO]

Q7: On a blank paper draw a picture of a sound wave signal?

Gases, Liquids and Solids

Key Stages 2 to 4

Investigation No: 8
To investigate the three states of matter.

Below tick the words which represents **GASES**:

a) Oxygen
b) Carbon
c) Soda
d) Carbon Dioxide
e) Water
f) CO_2
g) Iron
h) Hydrogen

Did You Know?

Solids, liquids and gases have different properties.

Liquids and gases can flow.
Solids keep their shape.
Gases can be squashed.

Below tick the words which represents **LIQUIDS**:

a) Oxygen
b) H_2O
c) Carbon
d) Coca Cola
e) Water
f) CO_2
g) Mercury

Did You Know?

If heated, solids can change to liquids, and liquids can change to gases.
If cooled the opposite can occur.
This is some times known as the:
Three States of Matter.

Below tick the words which represents **SOLIDS**:

a) Carbon
b) Coal
c) Electricity
d) CO_2
e) Fe
f) Hydrogen
g) Gold

Mathematics

Matching Numbers To Words

Key Stages 1 to 3

To practice addition, subtraction, multiplication and division.

Check your answers against the numbers in the code table on the next page and try to make the words below the code table match your answers.

20 +0 2 ___	10 +0 2 ___	0 3 +3 0 ___	2 2 +2 2 ___
2 3 +1 5 ___	5 3 +2 6 ___	4 3 +5 1 ___	8 7 +1 2 ___
0 1 2 +0 1 0 ___	1 3 2 +2 3 0 ___	4 2 6 +5 3 0 ___	4 5 1 +2 3 9 ___
6 4 -3 2 ___	3 3 -3 0 ___	7 9 -5 7 ___	7 3 -3 2 ___
9 3 -7 1 ___	1 0 0 -3 7 ___	1 6 0 -1 3 8 ___	8 0 0 -2 3 0 ___
1 3 x 2 ___	2 3 x 5 ___	0 3 x 3 4 ___	2 9 x 3 3 ___
10 ÷ 5 =	20 ÷ 10 =	100 ÷ 50 =	1000 ÷ 500 =

Code Table:

A	B	C	D	E	F	G	H	I	J	K	L	M
50	100	680	362	79 022	28	41	33	22 956	5	90	87	12 99

N	O	P	Q	R	S	T	U	V	W	X	Y	Z
63	44	94	11	71	26	38	570	27	31	40	25	400

Answers at bottom of page:

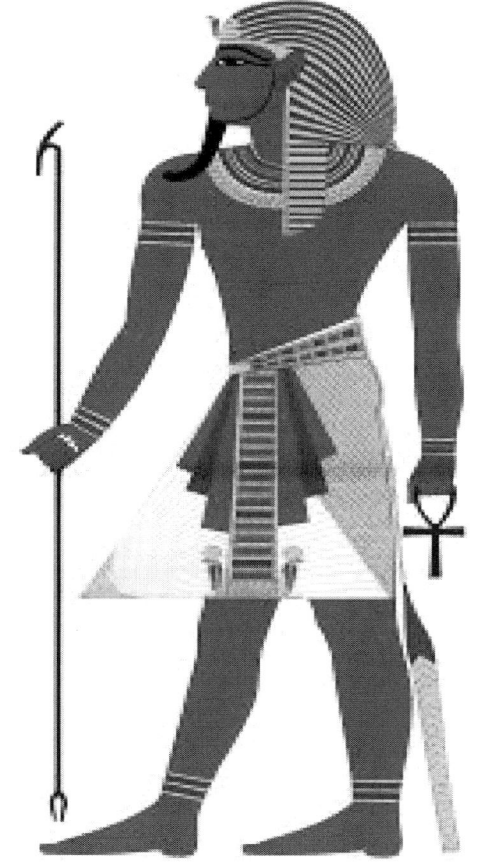

Ancient Egyptian Man

Imhotep, Medicine, Genius

Understanding Numbers

Key Stages 1 to 2

Place the numbers below in the correct columns in the table.

30, 1, 5, 20, 10, 100, 150, 99, 1000, 1500, 1600, 1609, 8, 1.000000, 5.000000. Two Million, Seven, Eleven, Two Hundred and Thirty, One Thousand and Twenty Three.

Million	Hundred Thousand	Ten Thousand	Thousand	Hundred	Ten	Unit
					3	0

Rivers of Africa, America and Europe.

Key Stages 2 to 3

Investigation No: 9

To investigate distances, addition and subtraction using rivers of our world.

Q1: The river Thames is the longest river in the UK, It is said to be: [   ] miles long.

Q2: The Volga river in Russia is the longest river in the Europe, It is said to be: [   ] miles long.

Q3: How much longer in miles is the Volga river compared to the river Thames?

Q4: The river Nile which runs through eleven countries in Africa is the longest river in the world. It is said to be: [   ] miles long.

Q5: The Amazon river is the second largest river in the world. It runs through six countries in South America. It is said to be: [   ] miles long.

Q6: How much longer is the river Nile compared to the Amazon river?

Did You Know?

The Nile which ends in Egypt, North Africa is believed to have its source in Lake Victoria. This large lake is shared by 3 African countries, they are: Uganda, Kenya and Tanzania.

Addition & Subtraction (+), (-)

Key Stages 2 to 3

Investigation No: 10

To investigate black scientists and inventors and practice addition and subtraction.

Q1: If Madame C.J. Walker was born in 1867 how old would she be today?

Q2: Emancipation was won by African Americans in 1865. How many years was this before Madam C.J. Walker was born?
Show how you reached your answer.

Q3: Granville T. Woods who was born in 1856 invented many electrical and mechanical devices, which included the **Carbon microphone**. The inventor James West who invented the **Electret microphone** was born in 1931.

a) Which inventor was born first?

b) What is the difference in their age?

c) If both inventors were alive today how old would they both be?

d) How much older is James West than you?[   ] and how much older is Granville T. Woods than you?[   ].

(Royalties) Percentages (%)

Key Stages 2 to 3

Investigation No: 11

To investigate Percentages and Royalties.

The **Super Soaker** ™ was invented by Lonnie Johnson in 1989, it is marketed and sold by Lamory Toys. The average sales price for one is £15.00 each.

Q1: If Lonnie receives 10% royalties from Lamory Toys for every Super Soaker ™ sold. How much does he receive if Lamory Toys sell one Super Soaker ™?

Q2: If 2,500.000 Super Soaker ™ are sold in one year, how much royalties does Lonnie receive for that year?

Q3: If the Super Soaker ™ sales improve the following year and now Lonnie's Super Soaker™ sell 5,000.000 units in that year, how much royalties does Lonnie receive for that year?

(**Clue:** *Look in Black Scientists & Inventors Books 6*)

Did You Know?

1. *Royalty* is a member of a royal family, but:
2. *Royalties* is an amount of money that is paid to the original inventor of a product, book, or piece of music based on how many copies have been sold.

Imhotep
Mathematics - Geometry

Key Stage 3

Investigation No: 12

To investigate the triangular shape and Africa's pyramids, sometimes referred to as the first wonder of the world. (**Clue:** *Look in Black Scientists & Inventors Books 2*)

Q1: What is a 2-dimensional shape pyramid called?

Q2: How many sides can be found on a 3-dimensional shaped pyramid?

Q3: The Greek mathematician Pythagoras was educated in Egypt, Africa and was born in approximately 570 BCE. Imhotep the African multi-genius was born approximately 2667 BCE.
Which of the two was born first?

Q4: What is the difference in age? (show how you got your answer).

Q5: The Greek doctor Hippocrates was born in approximately 460 BCE. Imhotep the African multi-genius was born approximately 2667 BCE. Which of the two was born first?

Q6: What is the difference in age? (show how you got your answer).

Q7: Modern day scientists have measured both the height and width of the step pyramid which the African multi-genius Imhotep designed in Egypt.
The scientists say that the base is 374 feet width long and that the height is 195 feet in height.

  a) If that is the case, what is the area of one side of that pyramid?
  b) What is the volume of the pyramid?

Q8: In order for a shape to be a triangle what must be the total of all angles when added together?

Financial Literacy

Financial Literacy:

Key Stages 1 to 2

Investigation No: 13

To investigate what money is.

Q1: What is MONEY?

Q2: Find out why goods (products) and services are usually exchanged for money?

Q3: Have you ever received money for work?
If yes describe the work you did, how you were paid and how did it make you feel?

Q4: In the old days, there were many different types of things used as money for the purpose of exchanging goods and services. Some are below.

Next to each one put the countries they were used in. You can ask an adult for help. You can also use both the internet and your local library to help you find the answers.

Item used as money	Country
Zappozats (decorated axes)	
Rice	
Salt	
Quartz	
Ivory	
Cowries	
Gold	
Wampum (beads on a string)	

Money Matters

Key Stages 2 to 4

Investigation No: 14

To investigate **CREDIT (Loans)** offered by a financial institution such as a bank.

What you will need:
For this exercise you will need to visit either your local bank, building society or credit union.

Method:
Ask the bank assistant for brochures on the following: Personal loans, Business loans, Cash card, Credit card, Debit card, Master card, Overdrafts and Mortgages. Read through the brochures, the parts you don't understand ask either the bank assistant, your parents or teachers to explain it to you.

Results:

a) What is a bank loan?
b) What is the difference between a business loan and a personal loan?
c) What is a mortgage?
d) Which type of bank account comes with overdraft facilities?
e) What is a debit card?
f) What is the difference between a cash card, debit card, credit card and master card?
g) What is bank interest and why do the banks apply it?

Percentage Interest on Loans

Q1: If the bank loans give you £1000.00, but requires you to pay it back as a one-off payment in 12 months time, but for this service they require you to pay an additional 15% interest on the loan.
How much will you have to pay in total ?

Q2: The bank also tells you that if you miss the payment in 12 months time, even by one day, you will have to pay back the loan plus 25% instead of 15% interest. How much in total would you pay?

This page is left blank for notes.

Answers

Science Section

Page 14:
Q1 = Red, Q2 = Blood consists of blood plasma which is a yellowish liquid that carries nutrients, hormones, and proteins throughout the body.
Q3 = Red blood cell, White blood cell, Q4 = Charles Richard Drew

Page 15:
Q1 = Professor Charles Ssali, Q2 = 1992, Q3 = Answer found in Black Scientists & Inventors Book 3

Page 17:
Q1 = Lewis H. Latimer, Q2 = Garrett A. Morgan, Q3 = Imhotep, Q4 = Africa, Q5 = African builders, Q6 = Lewis H. Latimer, Q7 = Africa, 3000 BCE.

Page 19:
Q1 = Water, Light and Carbon Dioxide., Q2 = Jamaica, Ghana, Tanzania, Q3= Sugar Cane
Q4 = Barbados, St Vincent.

Page 20:
Q1 = A veterinary, Q2 = Either a veterinary physician, a veterinarian or vet., Q6 = the science of breeding and caring for farm animals., Q7 = A horse is larger than a zebra and a Zebra fur has the colours white and black, Zebras don't have a hairy tail like a horse does and their mane always sticks straight up., Q8 = Africa

Page 21:
Q1 = Radio, Mobile phone, electric kettle, light bulb., Q2 = Clouds.
Q1 = No, Q2 = No, Q3 = No, Q4 = No, Q5 = Yes, Q6 = Yes.

Mathematics Section

Page 27:
Q1 = 346 km, Q2 = 3,692 km , Q3 = 3346 , Q4 = 6,853 km , Q5 = 6,992 km , Q6 = According to new scientific research the Amazon is now longer than the Nile by 139 Km

Page 28:
Q1 = in the year 2016 Walker would be 149 years old, Q2 = 2 years, Q3 a = Granville T. Wood, Q3 b = 75 years, Q3 c = Woods 160 years old, West 85 years old.

Page 29:
Q1 = £1.50 , Q2 = £250,000, Q3 = £500000

Page 30:
Q1 = Triangle, Q2 = 5 sides, Q3 = Imhotep, Q4 = 2097 Years, Q5 = Imhotep, Q6 = 2207, Q7a = A=30615, Q7b = in order to get the answer you need to also know the length of its length, Q8 = 180 degrees.

Financial Literacy Section

Page 33:
Q1 = 1150, Q2 = 1250.

Pocket answer section for SQA English Intermediate 2
1999 SQP, 2000 to 2002 Exams, 2003 SQP and 2003 Exam

© 2003 Scottish Qualifications Authority, All Rights Reserved
Published by Leckie & Leckie Ltd, 8 Whitehill Terrace, St Andrews, Scotland, KY16 8RN
tel: 01334 475656, fax: 01334 477392, enquiries@leckieandleckie.co.uk, www.leckieandleckie.co.uk

English Intermediate 2
Paper I: Interpretation
1999 Specimen Question Paper

1. Appeals to common experience
   Conversational/humorous tone
   Refers directly to the reader ("you"/"your")

2. Effective gloss of "a pair . . . coveted" (lines 4-7)
   e.g. The shoes bought, while not as expensive as those the child wanted cost more than the parent had intended to pay.

3. In disobeying the rules:
   of parents
   of school (in disobeying "rules")

4. (a) Idea of force/intensity
       Idea of humour
   (b) Any reasonable answer suggesting they are against uniforms/think it a strange idea/think it unnecessary/etc.
   (c) Wearing trainers is unhealthy/smelly/etc.

5. (a) Answers must cover:
       the advent of tartan tracks leading to more injuries
       the discovery of the cause of the injuries
       the design of new footwear to reduce injuries
   (b) Gloss of the first sentence in paragraph 6, "Yet . . . track"
   (c) Gloss of "cult figures"
       Examples from sport/music
       Gloss of "to wear . . . 'totally sad' "

6. Answers should comment on the balanced nature of the paragraph.
   The first part deals with the advantages of tartan tracks;
   the last part deals with the disadvantages;
   the effect of the pivotal sentence beginning "But . . ."

7. Answers should identify three effective words/expressions and make sensible comment on their appropriateness/effectiveness in context

8. Gloss of paragraph 12
   Gloss of paragraph 13

9. Quote/reference + valid comment

10. (a) Explanation of humorous effect created
        Explanation of relevance in context
    (b) Valid feature identified
        Explanation of appropriateness to purpose

11. Explain the meaning of/comment on the appropriateness/inappropriateness of "rues" "put the boot into family budgets."
    [Comments on the appropriateness of the register/tone of the by-line]

English Intermediate 2
Paper II
1999 Specimen Question Paper

Analysis

1. Idea of contrast or development between the two sections
   Actions, fun, activity, anticipation of the actual picking
   Anti-climax/moral/lesson/disappointment/guilt/greed/generalisation

2. unripe: hard as a knot
            red ones inked up
   ripe: glossy purple clot
            flesh (was sweet)
            summer's blood . . . stains
            lust for picking

3. In each case:
   Explanation of connotation(s)
   Explanation of relationship with sensual world of childhood

4. "dark blobs burned like a plate of eyes"—some idea of accusation
   "palms sticky as Bluebeard's"—some idea of guilty blood

5. identification of technique with reference/explanation of effect

Appreciation

6. (a) Any sensible answer—most probably to do with making personal/creating sympathy/self identification
   (b) explanation of simple meaning
       effectiveness as conclusion
       identification of technique (rhyme/sentence structure/syntax of last line/enjambment)
       explanation of effectiveness in conclusion

7. This is a mini critical essay asking for personal response, comment on techniques and an understanding of the message of the poem.

Critical Essay

See pages 5 to 6 for answers to Critical Essay

English and Communication
Intermediate 2
Interpretation 2000

1. Indication that the tone/style/register is colloquial/informal + example of colloquial language

2. (a) He is active at night
   (b) Explanation of the idea conveyed by "Eternal nocturnal—too much of a good thing" (lines 42–43) i.e. he is trapped in perpetual/continuous dark and therefore unable to sleep
   (c) **Any two from**:
   They eat cockroaches/insects
   They eat small mice
   They have poor eyesight
   Their hairs are sensitive to sound

3. Saunter
   ["I love the . . . shadows . . . dark places . . . dappled murk]

4. **Any two from**:
   He knows the cinema very well (line 8)
   The passage implies he goes to the cinema every night (lines 8–9)
   Has a favourite seat (line 10)
   His ability to quote favourite lines from films (lines 16–18)
   Only leaves after the last show (lines 38–39)
   Comments he makes on "Kilimanjaro"
   He knows the names of the stars

5. (a) He doesn't like it (however the idea is expressed)
   reference to/gloss of "No Oscars for this baby"
   or appropriate comment on the implications of "seen it, seen it, and seen it"
   or idea that the only good scene involves the tarantula
   or the improbability of the plot
   (b) "and that speaks to me" (line 51)
   (c) Use of " . . . there—right there—"
   or Expression "I couldn't believe it"/"It was one of us—one of me" (lines 64/65)
   (d) His looks

6. (a) From admiration of the "star" to anger at, exasperation/impatience with the audience
   (b) Any appropriate structural feature (Use of "minor" incomplete/non-sentence, use of ellipsis, use of repetition/listing) + explanation
   Any appropriate comment on word choice [(contrast between) connotations of "grace" "elegance" "lovely smile" and "disgusted" "revolted" etc] + explanation, implications of "They" + explanation

7. (a) The serpent or snake
   (b) Gloss of fangs (teeth) and venom (poison)

8. **Any three from:**
   The fact that they were able to train the spider in the film
   The fact that a tarantula bite is no stronger than a hornet sting, (but hornets are less hated)
   The fact that human hunting/eating habits are no better than tarantula eating habits
   Tarantulas only kill when they are hungry
   A man could . . . never bite him
   The bite is not life-threatening

9. (a) (Highly developed) sense of touch
   (b) Quote an appropriate expression (which must relate to the answer given in (a))
   Explain its effectiveness e.g. "tarantula tactile"
   The alliteration on the letter "t" emphasises the idea of touch

10. Candidates are likely to argue that the paragraph rounds off the passage effectively because it draws together elements touched on earlier
    TWO ways should be identified in which lines 147–162 echo points from previous paragraphs **or** one way **FULLY SUPPORTED BY DETAILED EVIDENCE**

11. 1. anthropomorphism/personification helps us identify with the spider/see things from his point of view
       persona created is likeable + evidence
    2. quotation of effective expression
       + appropriate explanation of relevance to purpose
    3. identification of feature of structure/syntax
       + appropriate explanation of relevance to purpose
    4. identification of one of the techniques of argument
       + appropriate explanation of relevance to purpose
    5. quotation of expression creating an identified tone/register/style
       + appropriate explanation of its relevance to purpose
    6. example of humour
       + appropriate explanation of relevance to purpose

English and Communication
Intermediate 2
Analysis and Appreciation 2000

Part 1—Textual Analysis

1. (a) Reference to: jumbled/mud-smeared/peeling/grey/thin/leaning sideways/at an angle **or** to: cumulative effect of using many of these descriptions together

    With comment on their contribution to the unpleasantness

   (b) Long sentences
    suggests long time/stretches of water/slow progress **or**
    Repetition of "They passed"
    suggests length of time/length of journey/never ending
    quality of journey

2. Long sentence/long list of items giving impression of size/threat/decay/the idea of increasing tension or fear

   Short sentence(s) makes her seem small/insignificant/dominated/threatened

3. (a) Mystery/threat/other similar suggestion

   (b) Explanation of comparison suggested by the simile
    e.g. the shadow, or the lack of familiarity of the face made it difficult to see or hidden and therefore difficult to relate to, welcome or trust

   (c) Specific words:
    weathered/faded/poison/shadow/black/smoke/intimidating/evil
    Any **two** single words
    Explanation of connotations of at least one example

4. (a) **Connotations** of sliding/gently **or** **Explanation** of the simile

   (b) Reference
    1. the gift of a cauliflower
    2. bristly rush
    3. kiss
    4. delivered (like a parcel)

    Aspect
    1. generosity (or meanness)
    2. shyness/awkwardness
    3. affection
    4. care—or lack of care

5. Dishevelled appearance
   Cauliflower not usual luggage for a hotel visit
   Arriving on foot/carrying her own luggage—not usual
   Asking for a library
   Any **two** of the above

6. The decision is to buy Prince Rupert's Glassworks
   Pointers to that:
   Opening sentence of paragraph 5
   Information about her from introduction – money and/or independence
   glass is going to be important for her

7. (a) Reference to: self consciously
    all . . . looking at her
    ignorance about transport (omnibuses etc)
    cauliflower clutched (as if she must hang on to her gift or as if she doesn't know what to do with it)
    blushed brightly
    other sensible reference
    one reference with a comment on its effectiveness

   (b) Details of personality:
    nervousness
    home sickness
    stoicism
    decisiveness
    independence
    physical hardihood
    lack of vanity
    single mindedness
    studiousness
    other sensible aspects
    Any **two** of the above aspects with appropriate references.

Part 2—Critical Essay

See pages 5 to 6 for answers to Critical Essay

English and Communication
Intermediate 2
Close Reading 2001

1. Answers must cover the idea that visitors are keen to use them, because of the glamour attached to them by TV programmes and residents dislike them intensely as they are dangerous/uncomfortable

   There must be some attempt to gloss

2. The humour/hyperbole/exaggeration/absurdity of the first sentence/the blunt simplicity of the second sentence/the contrast between the two
   Any **one**

3. (a) Gloss of lines 7–8, "Even though everyone knows that the subway will be the first target of terrorists it's still safer than taking a cab"
    e.g. Though terrorists are more likely to attack subways travelling by cab is still more dangerous.

3. (b) Gloss of any two points from lines 9–10, e.g. He was carrying a lot of shopping, didn't want to struggle through the crowds

there was no sunshine in the underground

the surroundings were depressing.

(c) The answer expected is "cruise" because of its connotations of relaxation/ease of movement/(boating holidays)

But candidates may make a case for some other **single word**.

4. (a) For one mark candidates should suggest the idea that they don't get on/are contemptuous of each other/etc.

The other mark should be awarded for appropriate comment on the significance of any of "my **usual** grumbling act"

"the kind of glare **I've come to know** well"

"I am **accustomed** to rude arrogant passengers"

"not part of the deal"

(b) Lift or gloss of "he began talking"

5. (a) Explanations should suggest that "alternative reality" sounds more exotic and therefore is more appropriate to the unusual/exaggerated/fantastic/glamorous quality of the driver's imaginary existence.

or that it sounds more mocking and the writer thinks the driver is fooling himself

or that it sounds more American and so suits the setting

(b) One mark each for two facts that show his experiences had not been as glamorous as he thinks. E.g. He only came second in the Battle of the Bands/

He did not make a video with real stars but with people who looked like film stars/

He didn't really make a Swatch commercial/

He was not the subject of a magazine article, merely mentioned in it/etc.

(c) Appropriate comment on the use of colloquial language/the phrases Joe used/the characteristic expressions/repetitions/the emphasis he used etc.

6. (a) These phrases are more elevated/"posher"/"more formal" **or** most of the passage is colloquial/informal

(b) The fact that Eddie/Joe had not been able to do what he wanted to do in life **or** he had accepted a less glamorous job than he had hoped for is an example of an ambition that had not been fulfilled "i.e. some suggestion of the meaning of the quotation + an illustration of its truth from Joe's story"

7. (a) The idea that they can motivate people

They can make up for or compensate for reality

They can become an obsession.

Any **one**

7. (b) One mark for the idea of depth/conviction of belief suggested by "tenacious" (line 51) OR for the idea that accepting fate is an un-American spirit.

8. One mark for appropriate point, e.g.

Punchline quality/humour

Fact that it is a single sentence paragraph makes it stand out

The driver was not only fooling himself, he was fooling/conning the writer

Appropriate return to mundane customer/driver relationship etc.

9. Identification of a technique, example and full explanation of how it helps the writer entertain the reader OR give a flavour of New York life. Two techniques must be discussed.

English and Communication Intermediate 2
Analysis and Appreciation 2001

Part 1—Textual Analysis

1. cassettes—typical student more interested in music than anything else

toothbrush/paste/razor—essential for personal cleanliness or—not regarded as important (shoved in the side pockets) or taking care of them/leaving them at hand asthma/hay fever tablets—has weaknesses or feels anxious and takes them/is responsible etc. hairdryer—not vain/considerate/leaves it for his mother/grandmother.

2. (a) dark/dull/gloomy/old fashioned

(b) always dark/dull beyond belief/huge wardrobe/sickens/utterly/rid of

any two plus some comment on connotation

3.

Possible sentence structure features	
Funny–one word sentence	suggests stopping to think just as an idea comes into his head
verbless next sentence–	which appeals to him as he speculates on his new surroundings, and what they might contain
note form–	
repetition of practical–	
list of items–	
Short last sentence–	a satisfactory summing up
Possible punctuation features	
dash after practical–	waiting for its definition
colon after practical–	waiting for an expansion/definition of his thoughts of what practical might be
use of commas to construct list–	see above for possible comment
Identification of feature + comment	

4. impersonal/institutional/anonymous/part of residence/one of many/functional/clinical

5. firmly/(face) breaks/(from the) strain/hurriedly/stuffing/quickly
   any **one** with reason

6. succession of "and"—one after another/no spaces/no paragraphs/lack of full stops/other sensible answer
   Identification of feature + full comment

7. they both watch it with horror and it seems to take a long time to reach the floor/
   to give the impression that they were helpless to do anything about it/
   to draw attention to the importance and horror of the moment/
   like a slow motion sequence to create drama/inevitability

8. (a) to avoid prolonged goodbyes
   (b) The problem is . . . (line 8)
       No point . . . (line 9)
       cheeks wet . . . somehow shrunken (lines 24-25)
       out the door running . . . (line 32)
       other sensible choice
       Reference plus explanation

9. N.B. <u>significant detail</u>—<u>how successful</u>
   Choice of detail about the character + a comment dealing with the success of the language used in revealing feelings

10. (a) Its breaking is a symbol of the severing/weakening of the bond between boy and his grandparents
        It marks the end of something/a period in one's life (his or the grandparents)
        It reflects the pain of separation
        Other sensible answer—this is a very open question looking for some understanding of the symbolic nature of the vase (not necessarily in those words).
    (b) title of story/dramatic short sentence "Her wedding gift."/graphic description of its falling/the grandmother's or the boy's reaction to the event/he tells us that it was a wedding gift/pride of place.

English and Communication Intermediate 2 Critical Essay 1999 Specimen Question Paper, 2000 and 2001

Part 2—Critical Essay

Materials should be read to establish that they meet the minimum standards of "sufficient accuracy". There is obviously a need for a professional interpretation of this definition. Expression must meet all the required standards.

Essays should be read then to see whether the work attains success in terms of all the Performance Criteria—if it attains all, a C pass has been achieved. When minimum standards are not achieved a mark up to a maximum of 14 can still be awarded.

At this stage, the supplementary marking grid will allow you to place the work on a scale of marks out of 30.

Core Skills

Core skills will be achieved when, in Paper 2 Critical Essay, the writer consistently, in continuous prose, responds to a question, by writing about a text previously studied.

Spelling, syntax and punctuation will be sufficiently accurate to satisfy the standards of formal competence.

Sufficiently accurate: demands professional judgement with respect to the following, making allowance for speed and the lack of opportunity to redraft.

Grade C—Performance Criteria

(a) **Understanding**

As appropriate to task, the response demonstrates understanding of key elements, central concerns and significant details of the text(s).

(b) **Analysis**

The response explains in some detail ways in which aspects of structure/style/language contribute to meaning/effect/impact.

(c) **Evaluation**

The response reveals engagement with the text(s) or aspects of the text(s) and stated or implied evaluation of effectiveness, substantiated with some relevant evidence from the text(s).

(d) **Expression**

Structure, style and language, including use of some appropriate critical terminology, are deployed to communicate meaning clearly and develop a line of thought which is generally relevant to purpose; spelling, syntax and punctuation are sufficiently accurate.

English and Communication Intermediate 2 Critical Essay—Supplementary Advice

IV 11–14	III 15–18	II 19–23	I 24–30
Responses which fall into this category may do so for a variety of reasons. It could be: that it **fails to achieve sufficient technical accuracy*** or that any knowledge and understanding of the text is **not deployed** as a response relevant to the task or that analysis and evaluation attempted are **unconvincing** or that the answer is **simply too thin** **Insufficient attention** to **the purpose** of the task * See note on **Core Skills**	**Understanding** **Knowledge** of the text, and an understanding of the **main concerns** of the text(s) will be used to provide a **generally relevant** response to the task. **Some** reference to the text will be made to **support** the candidate's argument.	**Understanding** **Knowledge and an understanding** of the **central concerns** of the text(s) material will be used to provide an answer which is **relevant** to the task. **Reference** to the text will be used as evidence **to promote** the candidate's argument.	**Understanding** **Secure knowledge and some insight** into the **central concerns** of the text(s) will be demonstrated at this level and there will be a **line of thought clearly and consistently** relevant to the task. **Clear reference** to the text will be used **appropriately** as evidence which helps **to develop** the argument fully.
	Analysis There will be **an explanation** of the contribution of techniques to the **impact** of the text(s).	**Analysis** There will be a **clear explanation of the effectiveness** of the contribution of techniques to the **impact** of the text(s).	**Analysis** There will be **some insight shown into the effectiveness** of the contribution of techniques to the **impact** of the text(s).
	Evaluation There will be some **engagement** with the text(s) which will state or **imply an evaluation** of its effectiveness.	**Evaluation** There will be **clear engagement** with the text which leads to **a generally valid evaluative stance** with respect to the text(s).	**Evaluation** There will be a **clear and consistent** engagement with the text(s) which leads to **a valid evaluative stance** with respect to the text(s).
	Expression Language will **communicate the argument clearly**, and there will be **appropriate critical terminology** deployed. Spelling, syntax and punctuation will be **sufficiently accurate**.	**Expression** Language will **communicate the argument clearly**, and there will be **appropriate critical terminology** deployed **to support the argument**. Spelling syntax and punctuation will be **sufficiently accurate**.	**Expression** The language will **communicate effectively** making **appropriate and effective use of critical terminology to further the argument**. Spelling syntax and punctuation will be **sufficiently accurate**.

English & Communication Intermediate 2
Close Reading 2002

1. What he was reading frightened/shocked/surprised him
    or
    the late hour/tiredness

2. Full explanation of the humour created by the contrast between the formality of "clinically precise" (dispassionately, objectively, impassively or medically exact) and the informality/horror of "gnawed pulpy"

3. (a) Any suggestion that it is an aside
    (b) Any suggestion that it suggests the writer's surprise

4. (a) smell/aroma
    (b) "olfactory"

5. Gloss of "round a bend . . . appraisingly" (lines 9–10)
    e.g. by being unlucky enough to bump into one on the trail
    Gloss of "wander unwittingly . . . prey"
    e.g. by meandering/walking into the area dominated by/the domain of/an old/injured bear

6. (a) **Any three from**
    Grizzlies don't hunt/roam beyond the west bank of the Mississippi
    Black bears outnumber grizzlies
    There is an increased number of/there are a great many black bears in the country (as a whole)
    There are many black bears in the area the writer was going to visit
    Grizzlies in USA are confined to one area
    (b) Gloss of "retiring" (line 28)
    e.g. They are shy

7. Labelled is more appropriate to a scientific specimen

8. The alliteration on the letter "p" suggest pricking/puncturing
    or
    The image of the porcupine is appropriate to something covered in arrows
    or
    The humourous image suits the tone of the passage
    or
    Porcupine used as verb is unusual

9. Technique identified/example given + explanation
    or
    [Relevant point about structure or example + explanation
    or
    Relevant point about word-choice or example + explanation
    or
    Relevant point about punctuation or example + explanation]

10. Skilful/adept/able/expert/etc.
    The fact that the writer says it is foolish to try to escape a black bear by climbing a tree/the fact that you could end up fighting a black bear in a tree suggests black bears can climb well

11. (a) Make a lot of noise
    Throw things at it
    Run at the bear
    Any two
    (b) "Yeah, right"/"you first, Professor"/"Well thanks"

12. To demonstrate/illustrate the unpredictability of bear behaviour/unreliability of the advice

13. Relevant technique identified in passage explanation of contribution to popularity/how it works

English & Communication Intermediate 2
Analysis and Appreciation 2002

Part 1—Textual Analysis

1. (a) Touch
    (b) scrap of doormat (with claws)
    or
    scrubbing brush (with teeth)
    Explanation of image (i.e. the feel of rough fur like the roughness of a doormat or the teeth adding to the sudden realisation that it is not a doormat, therefore horrible)
    (c) the leaves/old sacks give impression of rubbish/unpleasant litter which makes the discovery even more disgusting
    or
    world's most unlit outhouse—reference to the darkness adding to the unknown and therefore more terrifying
    or
    outhouse—idea of remote, forsaken, isolated and thus leaving the feeling of being unsupported, afraid . . .

2. (a) he gasps, gulps air . . .
    (b) imagery
    bellows/like a hunting thing/breath rushes into me
    word-choice
    bellow/sucks/rushes/hunting (thing)/scared
    Comment required for each

3. it is hard/mummified

English & Communication
Intermediate 2
Analysis and Appreciation 2002 (contd.)

4. Pebble is inanimate therefore cannot ever have been alive

5. (a) Were you taken by surprise?

   (b) suggests they have been part of an endless battle—humans against vermin

   or

   suggests close relationship between them

   or

   the phrase suggests a subconscious echo of "old friend"

6. line 13—literal
   line 18—use of different meaning/pun/metaphorical and explanation

7. (a) the sight of the rat's eye socket/empty eye/eye

   (b) repetition—eyeless/eye/fullstop/stops/mid-life/mid thought
   enjambement—fullstop—stop
   punctuation—dashes
   alliteration—mid-life/mid-thought/riddle . . . reminds
   imagery—riddle
   and how it makes the moment dramatic

8. uses repetition "out (of my mind's) out (of sight)" to signify the completeness of the rejection

   or

   odd use of possessive in "mind's"—showing the mind's desire to forget . . . ?

   or

   hyphenation of "out-of-sight" to create a new concept—a place where the rat could be thrown

   or

   reversal of cliché "out of sight out of mind"

9. Ideas:
   Any answer that comes up with the inevitability of death or the fact that man and rat are equally mortal
   Word choice
   grinning—rat has last laugh
   like to like—equality in the face of death
   delicate (skeleton)—transformation of the ugliness/toughness of the body in the opening of the poem to the beauty/fragility of the skeleton
   fragility—not strong enough to keep death at bay

Part 2—Critical Essay

Marking Principles for Critical Essay are as follows:

- Essays should first be read to establish whether the essay achieves success in **all** the Performance Criteria for Grade C, including relevance and the standards for technical accuracy outlined in Note 1 below

- If minimum standards are not achieved in any **one** or more of the Performance Criteria, the maximum mark which can be awarded is 14.

- If minimum standards have been achieved then the supplementary marking grids will allow you to place the work on a scale of marks out of 30.

Notes

1. Technical Accuracy

- *Consistently accurate*: A few errors may be present, but these will not be significant in any way. The writer may use some complex vocabulary and sentence structures. Where appropriate, sentences will show accurate handling of clauses. Linking between sentences will be clear. Paragraphing will reflect a developing line of thought.

  Sufficiently accurate: As above but allowance for speed and the lack of opportunity to redraft.

2. Using the Category descriptions

- Categories are not grades. Although derived from performance criteria at C and the indicators of excellence for Grade A, the four categories are designed primarily to assist with placing each candidate response at an appropriate point on a continuum of achievement. Assumptions about final grades or association of final grades with particular categories should not be allowed to get in the way of objective assesment.

- Once an essay has been deemed to pass the criteria, it does not have to meet all the suggestions for, say, Category 2 to fall into that Category. More typically there will be a spectrum of strengths and weaknesses which span categories.

Grade C
Performance Criteria

(a) *Understanding*
As appropriate to task, the response demonstrates understanding of key elements, central concerns and significant details of the text(s).

(b) *Analysis*
The response explains in some detail ways in which aspects of structure/style/language contribute to meaning/effect/impact.

(c) *Evaluation*
The response reveals engagement with the text(s) or aspects of the text(s) and stated or implied evaluation of effectiveness, substantiated by some relevant evidence from the text(s).

(d) *Expression*
Structure, style and language, including use of some appropriate critical terminology, are deployed to communicate meaning clearly and develop a line of thought which is generally relevant to purpose; spelling, syntax and punctuation are sufficiently accurate.

It should be noted that the term "text" encompasses printed, audio or film/video text(s) which may be literary (fiction or non-fiction) or may relate to aspects of media or language.

Intermediate 2 Critical Essay Supplementary Advice

This advice, which is supplementary to the published Performance Criteria is designed to assist with the placing of scripts within the full range of marks. However, the Performance Criteria as published give the primary definitions. The mark range for each grade is identified.

IV 11–14	III 15–18	II 19–23	I 24–30
• Essays which fall into this category may do so for a variety of reasons. It could be • that it fails to achieve sufficient technical accuracy • or that any knowledge and understanding of the material is not deployed as a response relevant to the task • or that analysis and evaluation attempted are unconvincing • or that the answer is simply too thin.	**Understanding** • Knowledge of the text(s), and an understanding of the **main** concerns will be used. • to provide an answer which is **generally relevant** to the task. • Some reference to the text(s) will be made to **support** the candidate's argument.	**Understanding** • Knowledge and understanding of the **central** concerns of the text(s) will be used. • to provide an answer which is **mainly** relevant to the task. • Reference to the text(s) will be used as evidence to **promote** the candidate's argument.	**Understanding** • **Secure** knowledge **and some insight** into the central concerns of the text(s) will be demonstrated at this level. • and there will be a line of thought **consistently relevant** to the task. • Reference to the text(s) will be used **appropriately** as evidence which helps to **develop** the argument **fully**.
	Analysis • There will be an **explanation** of the contribution of literary/linguistic techniques to the impact of the text(s).	**Analysis** • There will be an **explanation of the effectiveness** of the contribution of literary/linguistic techniques to the impact of the text(s).	**Analysis** • There will be **some insight** shown into the **effectiveness** of the contribution of literary/linguistic techniques to the impact of the text(s).
	Evaluation • There will be **some engagement** with the text(s) which will state or imply an evaluation of its effectiveness.	**Evaluation** • There will be **engagement** with the text(s) which leads to a **generally valid** evaluative stance with respect to the text(s).	**Evaluation** • There will be a **clear engagement** with the text(s) which leads to a **valid** evaluative stance with respect to the material.
	Expression • Language will communicate the argument clearly, and there will be appropriate critical terminology deployed. Spelling, syntax and punctuation will be sufficiently accurate.	**Expression** • Language will communicate the argument **clearly**, and there will be appropriate critical terminology deployed **to aid the argument**. Spelling, syntax and punctuation will be sufficiently accurate.	**Expression** • The language will communicate **effectively** making appropriate use of critical terminology to further the argument. Spelling, syntax and punctuation will be sufficiently accurate.

English Intermediate 2
Close Reading
Specimen Question Paper
(in and after 2003)

1. Lift or gloss of "Jennifer doesn't expect us to" **or** To engage/establish rapport with the audience

2. It suggests that they may **actually** "provide straightforward answers", but people do not think they do
   Condensed answers e.g. People **only think** they do not provide straightforward answers are also acceptable

3. Answers should convey the idea of a long established organisation and cite an example given in the rest of the paragraph as the clue

4. (a) Expressions like "beware", "slick", "glossy", "superficial" suggest admen should be avoided/are underhand/artificial

   (b) Gloss of "(highly developed) spin detectors" eg the ability to see through propaganda/deception/brainwashing/biased publicity/etc.

5. (a) Gloss of lines 21–22
       e.g. They are (instinctively) good at explaining things to other scientists

   (b) Gloss of lines 23–25
       e.g. Ordinary scientists do not get the chance to explain things very often
       or
       only high up, important, promoted scientists ever get the chance to explain things

6. (a) To copy/repeat/parody the advert
       or
       To maintain the tone/humour
       or
       To link the elements of his argument

   (b) Mock indignation/humour
       Incomplete sentence/use of exclamation mark/hyperbole
       Any two

   (c) Ordinary people/amateurs/etc are replacing experts/people like him (in advertising/promoting/recommending things)

7. (a) C or "more difficult"

   (b) the word "gentler" suggests less demanding

8. The parallelism/repetition of "They"
   or
   The use of a very long sentence followed by several short ones
   creates a sense of climax
   or
   emphasises the similarity between scientists and ordinary people
   or
   suggests the ebb and flow of a discussion/argument

9. (a) Scientists invented it as a way for them to share information
       or
       Their exclusive communication system is now open to anyone

   (b) The selection of the argument implies being convinced by it
       The argument must be explained, not simply lifted

       e.g. From antepenultimate paragraph,
       Gloss of "the internet is no respecter of hierarchy" (e.g. I agree that people who use the internet don't care about status/think they're equal to anyone else/are more interested in what is said than who is saying it)
       or
       It's true that internet users like to get involved in chat rooms/tell each other about interesting sites—therefore the audience would grow

       Gloss of the penultimate paragraph, e.g.
       Though the ideas published on it will vary in quality and difficulty, people can handle this because they make decisions about what's worthwhile and what's not every day

       From the final paragraph
       He shows that even busy people have time to chat on the internet by giving an example
       or
       He says it is easy to set up a web page and that people like scientists, who already have degrees, would have no difficulty with it

       Answers must come from at least two of the final three paragraphs.

N.B. Please see pages 12 – 13 for the Critical Essay Paper

English Intermediate 2
Close Reading
2003

1. (a) He wanted to experience the river in detail

   (b) He could have camped out but stayed in hotels

2. (a) Acceptance by the river society/treated as an insider

   Knowledge of the jargon/ability to talk knowledgeably

   (b) "Lore"

3. "(I) wandered (down the...)"

   "...drank...too long"

   "(I could) gossip comfortably..."

   "(...easily able to) drift (into the lives...)"

   Any two

4. (a) He was glad to be rid of it/hadn't liked it (e.g. "dumped the unlovely...")

   He thought travelling by boat was too dangerous

   He thought travelling by boat was too much of a mental strain

   Any two

   (b) "(...unexpectedly) bereft"

   "(...remember with a) pang"

   Accept also "I'd lost the river and the boat", provided this is quoted separately from "pang"

   Any two

5. The repeated 's' sound conveys the gentle, leisurely nature of the outings.

6. (a) Adequate for basic living

   Appropriate speed for observing life

   Dangerous enough to keep you on your toes/provide excitement

   The enjoyment of being at the mercy of the weather

   Any two

   N.B. No credit will be given for straight lifts from the text.

   (b) Similar OR repeated pattern/like a list

   All start with the important part of the reason

   Minor/incomplete sentences

   Any two

   OR one of the above features plus an appropriate explanation of the effect, e.g. the repeated pattern of the list reinforces the strength of his feeling about living on the boat

7. **Sentence structure**
   "wind" placed at the beginning of the 2nd and 3rd sentences indicating its importance/repeated use of the word "wind"
   OR
   Balance of 4th and 5th sentences reflect the wind being in opposition to your desire

   Accept answers which argue that the rhythm created by the sentence structure/punctuation in the paragraph suggests unpredictability

   Imagery
   personification of the wind (pinioned/mad travel agent/malicious/maroon/consent/advice/driven)

8. "...Unpredictable business"/"finding yourself stranded"/"Gosfield Maid has taken me"/"landing the boat up"/"no idea I was destined to visit..."

   Any two

9. You may wish to consider any **one** feature such as structure, word-choice or illustration.

   Structure
   begins with "It" which is only explained after the colon
   OR
   comment on the final sentence, particularly after the dash

   Word-choice
   comment on, for example, "dingiest...wonderful"/ "humiliating"/"windfall-landfalls"

   Illustration
   comment on, for example, "kissing the stones of Grimsby..."

   N.B. No credit will be given for reference alone.

10. Identification of appropriate feature and full explanation of how well it helps the writer achieve his purpose.

    You may choose features identified in earlier questions, e.g. structure, word-choice, imagery, illustration.

    Other possible answers include the writer's use of:

    Example
    He mentions the many places he visited in order to convey the variety of experiences acquired through travelling by boat.

    1st person
    range of personal experiences covered, making clear his direct involvement

    2nd person
    creating a friendly tone which implies an informal pact between writer and reader/make the reader feel involved

    N.B. Please see pages 12–13 for the Critical Essay Paper

English Intermediate 2 Critical Essay Specimen Question Paper (in and after 2003) and 2003 Exam

Marking principles for Critical Essay are as follows

- Each essay should first be read to establish whether the essay achieves success in **all** the Performance Criteria for Grade C, including relevance and the standards for technical accuracy outlined in Note 1 below.
- If minimum standards are not achieved in any **one** or more of the Performance Criteria, the maximum mark which can be awarded is 11.
- If minimum standards have been achieved, then the supplementary marking grids will allow you to place the work on a scale of marks out of 25.
- The Category awarded and the mark should be placed at the end of the essay.

Notes

1. "Sufficiently accurate" can best be defined in terms of a definition of "consistently accurate".
   - *Consistently accurate*
     A few errors may be present, but these will not be significant in any way. The candidate may use some complex vocabulary and sentence structures. Where appropriate, sentences will show accurate handling of clauses. Linking between sentences will be clear. Paragraphing will reflect a developing line of thought.
   - *Sufficiently accurate*
     As above but with an allowance made for speed and the lack of opportunity to redraft.

2. Using the Category descriptions
   - Categories are not grades. Although derived from performance criteria at C and the indicators of excellence for Grade A, the four categories are designed primarily to assist with placing each candidate response at an appropriate point on a continuum of achievement. Assumptions about final grades or association of final grades with particular categories should not be allowed to influence objective assessment.
   - Once an essay has been deemed to pass the basic criteria, it does not have to meet all the suggestions for Category II (for example) to fall into that Category. More typically there will be a spectrum of strengths and weaknesses which span categories.

Grade C
Performance Criteria

(a) *Understanding*
As appropriate to task, the response demonstrates understanding of key elements, central concerns and significant details of the text(s).

(b) *Analysis*
The response explains in some detail ways in which aspects of structure/style/language contribute to meaning/effect/impact.

(c) *Evaluation*
The response reveals engagement with the text(s) or aspects of the text(s) and stated or implied evaluation of effectiveness, substantiated by some relevant evidence from the text(s).

(d) *Expression*
Structure, style and language, including use of some appropriate critical terminology, are deployed to communicate meaning clearly and develop a line of thought which is generally relevant to purpose; spelling, grammar and punctuation are sufficiently accurate.

It should be noted that the term "text" encompasses printed, audio or film/video text(s) which may be literary (fiction or non-fiction) or may relate to aspects of media or language.

Please see Page 13 for Critical Essay Supplementary Advice

Intermediate 2 Critical Essay Supplementary Advice

This advice, which is supplementary to the published Performance Criteria, is designed to assist with the placing of scripts within the full range of marks. However, the Performance Criteria as published give the primary definitions. The mark range for each Category is identified.

IV 8–11	III 12–15	II 16–19	I 20–25
• An essay which falls into this category may do so for a variety of reasons. It could be • that it fails to achieve sufficient technical accuracy • or that any knowledge and understanding of the material is not deployed as a response relevant to the task • or that analysis and evaluation attempted are unconvincing • or that the answer is simply too thin.	**Understanding** • Knowledge of the text(s), and a basic understanding of the **main** concerns will be used.	**Understanding** • Knowledge and understanding of the **central** concerns of the text(s) will be used.	**Understanding** • **Secure** knowledge **and some insight** into the central concerns of the text(s) will be demonstrated at this level.
	to provide an answer which is **generally relevant** to the task.	to provide an answer which is **mainly relevant** to the task.	and there will be a line of thought **consistently relevant** to the task.
	• Some reference to the text(s) will be made to **support** the candidate's argument.	• Reference to the text(s) will be used as evidence to **promote** the candidate's argument.	• Reference to the text(s) will be used **appropriately** as evidence which helps to **develop** the argument **fully**.
	Analysis • There will be an **explanation** of the contribution of literary/linguistic techniques to the impact of the text(s).	**Analysis** • There will be an **explanation of the effectiveness** of the contribution of literary/linguistic techniques to the impact of the text(s).	**Analysis** • There will be **some insight** shown into the **effectiveness** of the contribution of literary/linguistic techniques to the impact of the text(s).
	Evaluation • There will be **some engagement** with the text(s) which will state or imply an evaluation of its effectiveness.	**Evaluation** • There will be **engagement** with the text(s) which leads to a **generally valid** evaluative stance with respect to the text(s).	**Evaluation** • There will be a **clear engagement** with the text(s) which leads to a **valid** evaluative stance with respect to the material.
	Expression • Language will communicate the argument clearly, and there will be appropriate critical terminology deployed. Spelling, grammar and punctuation will be sufficiently accurate.	**Expression** • Language will communicate the argument **clearly**, and there will be appropriate critical terminology deployed **to aid the argument**. Spelling, grammar and punctuation will be sufficiently accurate.	**Expression** • The language will communicate **effectively** making appropriate use of critical terminology to further the argument. Spelling, grammar and punctuation will be sufficiently accurate.

Official SQA answers to 1-84372-112-0
2000 to 2003